NATURE CLOSE-UP

JUNIORS

Pond

TEXT BY ELAINE PASCOE

PHOTOGRAPHS BY DWIGHT KUHN

BLACKBIRCH PRESS

An imprint of Thomson Gale, a part of The Thomson Corporation

THOMSON

★

GALE

Detroit • New York • San Francisco • San Diego • New Haven, Conn. • Waterville, Maine • London • Munich

THOMSON

✦

GALE™

For more information, contact
Blackbirch Press
27500 Drake Rd.
Farmington Hills, MI 48331-3535
Or you can visit our Internet site at http://www.gale.com

Photo Credits: All pages © Dwight R. Kuhn Photography

LIBRARY OF CONGRESS CATALOGING-IN-PUBLICATION DATA

Pascoe, Elaine.
  Pond / text by Elaine Pascoe ; photographs by Dwight Kuhn.
    p. cm. — (Nature close-up jr.)
  Includes bibliographical references and index.
  ISBN 1-4103-0312-8 (hardcover : alk. paper)
  1. Pond ecology—Juvenile literature. I. Kuhn, Dwight, ill. II. Title III. Series: Pascoe, Elaine. Nature close-up junior.

  QH541.5.P63P384 2004
  578.763'6—dc22

                                                          2004015361

Printed in China
10 9 8 7 6 5 4 3 2 1

Contents

Read this first:

Have fun when you explore the pond, but be smart. Always take an adult with you. Walk carefully. Don't bother the animals that you see—just enjoy them.

Take a walk along the edge of a pond. Sunlight sparkles on the water. Lily pads float on the surface. A family of ducks swims by.

If you know where and how to look, you will see much more. The pond is full of living things. It is a great home, or **habitat**, for plants and animals. The plants and animals depend on each other. Together, they form a community.

Much of the life of the pond is hidden under the water. Many of the plants and animals are very small. You will have to look closely to see them.

Pond Plants

Lily pads are the big flat leaves of water lilies. They float on the pond surface. But their long stems go down to the bottom of the pond. Roots anchor the water lilies in the pond bottom.

Water lilies and other plants need sunlight to grow. They use the energy in sunlight to make their own food. A pond is shallow, so sunlight reaches all the way to the bottom. Plants can grow anywhere in a pond.

A water lily flower rises above the water of a pond.

Reeds grow near the shore. Pond weeds grow underwater. Clumps of duckweed float on the surface. Each duckweed plant has one tiny leaf. Its tiny roots hang free in the water.

You can find many kinds of **algae** in a pond, too. Algae are like plants but simpler. They do not have roots, stems, or leaves. But like plants, they make their own food.

Many algae are made up of just one **cell**. You may need a microscope to see them. But millions of algae cells may color or cloud the pond water. Some kinds of algae form clumps or long green strings.

Algae and plants are important to the pond. They are food for many of the animals that live here.

Top: Each tiny duckweed leaf is a separate plant. *Bottom:* Under a microscope, strands of algae look like green ropes.

Pond Plants Up Close

What You Need:
- Jar or other clear glass container
- Pond water

Study pond plants and algae up close by growing them at home.

Grow Pond Algae
- Dip some pond water into your jar. Take it home and put it on a sunny windowsill.
- Watch to see if algae grow. This may take a few weeks. You may see the water turn greenish. Or you may see thin green strands growing in the water.
- If you have a microscope, use it to look at some of the algae. Can you see the algae cells?

Grow Duckweed

- Dip some pond water into your jar.
- Gather some duckweed. These tiny plants float in clumps at the surface.
- Float one duckweed plant on the water in your jar. Take the jar home and put it on a sunny windowsill.
- Once a week, check the duckweed. See how it has changed. Make a drawing of it. How does the first plant make more plants? How fast does the duckweed grow?

Tiny Swimmers

Some pond animals are so small that you need a hand lens or a microscope to see them. Tiny water fleas are not really fleas. They belong to the same animal family as shrimp. But they seem to hop like fleas as they move through the water.

Copepods also belong to the shrimp family. "Copepod" means "oar foot." A copepod has paddle-like legs that it uses to swim. It has one eye, in the middle of its head. The copepod's eye is not very useful. It can sense light but not much else.

These little water animals eat even smaller living things, such as **bacteria** and tiny algae. And in turn they are food for larger animals.

Left: A water flea swims among algae. *Right:* This copepod is carrying eggs.

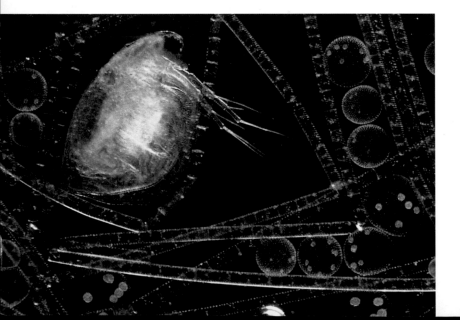

Pond Plant Bubbles

Pond animals must have oxygen to live. Some get oxygen the same way you do, by breathing air. But others get oxygen from the water.

Water plants help. They add oxygen to the water. Plants use the energy in sunlight to make food. They give off oxygen as they do this. You can see it happen with this activity.

What to do:
- Put some pond plants and water in the jar. Put water in the large bowl.
- Cover the jar and turn it upside down in the bowl. Then remove the top, keeping the water in the jar.
- Slide a few pennies under the rim of the upturned jar. This will allow water to flow in and out of the jar.
- Leave the bowl and jar in the sun for a few hours. Bubbles will form on the plants and float to the top of the jar. The bubbles are oxygen.

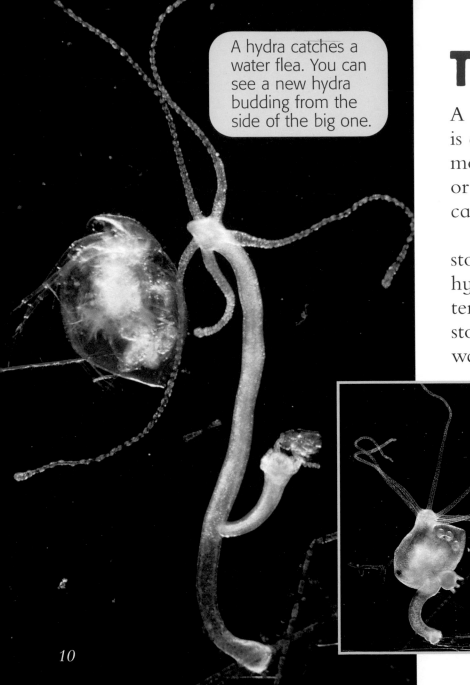

A hydra catches a water flea. You can see a new hydra budding from the side of the big one.

Tiny Stingers

A hydra looks like a tiny tube. Its mouth is at the open end of the tube. Around the mouth are as many as ten stinging arms, or tentacles. The hydra uses its arms to catch water fleas and other **prey**.

The hydra sticks itself to a plant or a stone. When a water flea swims near, the hydra grabs it and stings it with its tentacles. The sting makes the water flea stop moving. Then the hydra swallows the water flea whole.

Hydras are related to jellyfish. They are unusual in many ways. They **reproduce** by budding. That is, a new hydra grows from the side of an older hydra. If a hydra is cut in two, the parts will grow into two new hydras.

Left: The hydra has had its meal. Where is the water flea?

Hydra Hunt

Hydras are common in ponds. But they are often hard to see. Stretched out full length, a hydra may be 3/4 inch (about 2 cm) long. But if a hydra is bothered, it scrunches up into a tiny blob.

Here is a good way to find these little animals.

What You Need:
- Jar or other clear glass container
- Pond water
- Duckweed or other water plants

What to do:

- Scoop up some pond water in your jar.
- Gather duckweed or other water plants and put them in your jar. Hydras often live in these plants.
- Wait a few hours, and then check the jar. Hydras may have left the plants and attached to the sides of the jar. They may be green, gray, or brown.

If there are water fleas in your pond water, you may see a hydra catch its prey.

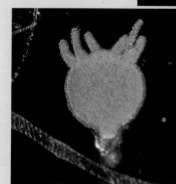

11

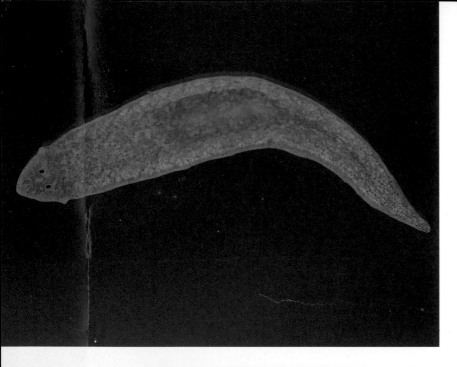

On the Bottom

Dead plants and wastes fall to the bottom of the pond. These materials slowly rot, forming layers of muck. And the muck is home to worms and other living things.

Small **flatworms** glide along in the muck. They eat dead material and sometimes tiny animals. The flatworm has two eyespots that can sense light. These worms do not like strong light. They spend a lot of time under rocks.

You may see other kinds of worms in the pond, too. Roundworms look like little bits of wiggly spaghetti. Leeches are small worms with a sucker at each end. Leeches latch onto fish and other animals. They feed by sucking the host animal's blood.

Top: Can you find this flatworm's eyespots?
Bottom: This leech is carrying eggs, which look like tiny beads. Can you see its suckers?

What's in the Muck?

The muck in the bottom of a pond is full of living things. Check it out.

What to do:

- Use the strainer or shovel to scoop up muck from the pond bottom.
- Put the muck on the plastic tray. Use the spoon or a stick to spread it out. Add a little water to thin it.
- Look carefully. Is anything moving? You can put the small animals in the jar of water to get a better look at them. Use your spoon to scoop them up—some little pond animals bite.
- Try to identify the animals. Compare them to the pictures in this book or in a field guide.

What You Need:

- Kitchen strainer or small shovel
- White plastic tray
- Small jar filled with clear water
- Spoon

13

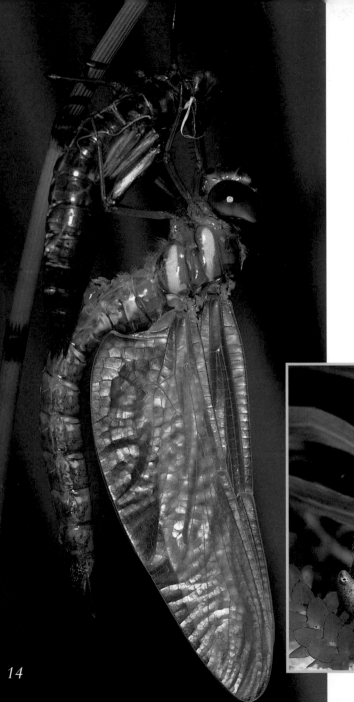

Dragonflies

A pond is full of crawling, wiggling things. Some are the young of insects like dragonflies. Dragonflies begin their lives as **nymphs** that live in the water.

The nymphs hatch from eggs. They are small at first. They have no wings. But they have six strong legs for swimming. They have strong jaws for catching and eating tiny water animals. And they have **gills** for breathing underwater. They do not need to come to the surface to breathe.

Like all insects, the nymphs have an outer shell. This shell does not grow. So, as a nymph grows, it must **molt**. It sheds its old shell and steps out in a new, bigger shell.

This dragonfly has just left its old nymph skin. *Inset:* Dragonfly nymphs are underwater hunters. This one has caught a tadpole.

With each molt, the nymph is a little more like an adult. Finally it crawls out of the water and molts one last time. Now it is an adult dragonfly. It spreads its wings. The wings quickly dry and stiffen in the air. Then the insect flies off.

Adult dragonflies are fierce hunters. They zoom over the pond surface, catching insects. They do not bother people.

Damselflies are a lot like dragonflies. Like dragonflies, they have long, skinny bodies and lacy wings. They, too, begin their lives in water. But as adults, they are not great fliers. Damselflies flutter. Dragonflies zip and dart.

Top: A dragonfly keeps its wings spread when it rests. *Bottom:* A damselfly folds its wings back when it rests.

Water Bugs

A giant waterbug is the biggest insect you are likely to see in a pond. These insects grow up to 4 inches (10 cm) long! They dive into the water to catch small fish, tadpoles, and other prey.

A giant waterbug cannot breathe underwater. So, when it dives, the waterbug carries along a bubble of air. The bubble is its air supply, like a scuba-diver's tank.

Waterbugs protect their eggs in an unusual way. The female lays her eggs on the male's back. Hungry fish will not bother the eggs there. A giant waterbug's bite is painful! It's best to leave these bugs alone.

Lots of other bugs live in and on the water. Water striders skate on the surface. Their long thin legs are tipped with tiny hairs that keep them afloat.

Backswimmers swim upside down. They are sometimes called water bees because their bites sting. Like the giant waterbug, these bugs are hunters. They mostly eat other insects.

A male giant waterbug carries the female's eggs on his back. *Inset:* Waterbugs dive to catch small fish like this minnow.

A backswimmer scoots through the pond water upside down.

17

More Pond Animals

Many other animals live in the pond. Small fish called minnows dart through the shallows. Bigger fish live in deeper water. Sunfish often hide among the water plants.

A turtle suns itself on a rock or a log at the pond's edge. When you come near, the turtle plops into the water and swims away. Most turtles are shy.

Turtles are land animals. But some, like the painted turtle, spend a lot of time in the water. The painted turtle eats snails, insects, and plants that it finds in the water. It uses its beak to slice its food.

Snails cannot move fast enough to escape a hungry fish or turtle. If danger threatens, the snail pulls its soft body inside its hard shell.

A painted turtle suns itself on a log. *Inset:* The pumpkinseed sunfish lives in many ponds.

Snail Study

Water snails creep along stones and plants in the pond. They eat algae and dead matter. Do you think these little animals like sunshine? Or will they hide from the sun? Here is an experiment that will help you find out.

What to do:

- Use your strainer to scoop up a water snail.
- Tip the snail into the flat container. Or use the spoon to move it.
- Add pond water to cover the snail.
- Cover half the container with dark cloth. Put the container in bright light.

Where does the snail go?

A Croaking Chorus

On spring nights a chorus of croaks fills the air around a pond. Male frogs are singing to attract mates.

Frogs belong to a group of animals called **amphibians.** Salamanders belong to this group, too. As adults, these animals live on land. But they begin their lives in water.

Frogs lay their eggs in water. The eggs hatch into tadpoles. Tadpoles do not look like frogs. They look like little fish. They have tails like fish. And they breathe water through gills, like fish.

Left: This tadpole is almost a frog. *Below:* Wood frogs mate in spring.

As a tadpole grows, its body slowly changes. It grows legs. Its tail shrinks. It develops lungs, to breathe air. Now it is ready to live on land, as an adult frog.

Frogs have powerful hind legs for jumping. They have **webbed feet** for swimming. And they have amazing tongues for catching prey. Frogs mostly eat insects and worms. When a frog sees a tasty insect, it flicks out its long, sticky tongue to grab it.

Frogs are **cold-blooded.** This means that their body temperatures change with the temperature of the air and water. To live through winter, some frogs dig into the mud at the bottom of ponds. They **hibernate** there until spring. Then they wake up and begin to croak.

A male spring peeper "peeps" in spring. He hopes a female will hear his song and come to his pond.

21

Words to Know

algae: simple living things that can make their own food using energy from sunlight.

amphibians: animals that spend part of their lives in water and part on land.

bacteria: simple living things with just one cell. Most are too small to see without a microscope.

cell: the basic unit of all living things. Simple living things may have one cell. You have millions of cells.

cold-blooded: having a body temperature that changes with the surrounding temperature.

flatworms: worms with flat bodies.

gills: body parts for breathing water.

habitat: the place where a plant or animal naturally lives.

hibernate: to rest in a deep sleep in which heart rate, breathing, and other body functions slow down.

molt: to shed the skin.

nymphs: the young forms of some insects. Nymphs often look like adults without wings.

prey: animals that are hunted by other animals

reproduce: to make more of one's kind.

webbed feet: feet with skin between the toes.

For More Information

Books

Emery Bernhard, *Dragonfly*. New York: Holiday House, 1993.

Diane L. Burns, *Frogs, Toads, and Turtles*. Milwaukee: Gareth Stevens, 2001.

Allan Fowler, *Life in a Pond*. Danbury, CT: Children's Press, 1996.

Anne Hunter, *What's in a Pond?* Boston: Houghton Mifflin, 1999.

George K. Reid, *Pond Life*. New York: St. Martin's Press, 2001.

Web Sites

Frogs (www.exploratorium.edu/frogs).
All about frogs, from the Exploratorium museum in San Francisco.

Habitat Guide: Lakes and Ponds (www.enature.com/habitats/show_sublifezone.asp?sublifezoneID=56).
This eNature.com site has links to online field guides for identifying pond plants and animals.

Pond Life Identification Kit and Virtual Pond Dip (www.microscopy-uk.org.uk/pond/).
Learn about some common types of small pond life, from *Micscape* magazine.

Index